Quiet Moments

with Young Children
Ages 6-8

by Jane B. Sorenson

illustrated by Diane Johnson

STANDARD PUBLISHING
Cincinnati, Ohio   12-02804

Cover Art by Richard D. Wahl

All Scripture quotations are from the Holy Bible, New International Version. Copyright ©1973, 1978, 1984 International Bible Society. Used by permission of Zondervan Bible Publishers.

Library of Congress Cataloging-in-Publication Data

Sorenson, Jane.
    Quiet moments with young children/by Jane B. Sorenson; illustrated by Diane Johnson.
        p. cm.
    Summary: Includes sixty devotions to help handle everyday situations involving fears, obedience, respect, forgiveness, self-control and praise.
    ISBN 0-87403-472-8
    1. Children—Prayer-books and devotions—English. [1. Prayer books and devotions.] I. Johnson, Diane, 1951-   ill. II. Title.
BV4870.S65   1988
242′.62—dc19   88-15903
                                                          CIP
                                                          AC

©1988 The STANDARD PUBLISHING Company, Cincinnati, Ohio.
A division of STANDEX INTERNATIONAL Corporation.
Printed in U.S.A.

Contents

All About You

1

What God Says:

I praise you because I am fearfully and wonderfully made; your works are wonderful, I know that full well.
Psalm 139:14

I think about it:

"My nose is too big!" Sharon said.

"Too big for what?" her mother asked. "Is it too big for smelling? Is it too big for breathing?"

"It looks funny," Sharon said. "You know, too big."

"It doesn't look too big to me," her mother said. "Does it cover up your eyes so you can't see? Does it cover up your mouth so you can't eat or talk?"

By now Sharon was laughing. "I guess God made it just right for me," she said.

*   *   *   *   *

Computers are pretty amazing. But does even the most

intricate computer compare with a human body? Did you "just happen"?

My response:

Have you thanked God for creating you exactly the way He wanted you?

What's Your Name?

2

What God Says:

"Fear not, for I have redeemed you; I have called you by name; you are mine."

Isaiah 43:1

I think about it:

Steve and Linda Campbell were in the back seat when a policeman pulled their mother over to the curb. "Let me see your driver's license," he said.

"Oh, no," Mrs. Campbell said. She sounded scared. "I didn't bring my purse. We're going to the swimming pool, and I didn't want to leave it in the basket."

The policeman stood there and looked at her. "What's your name?" he asked. Mrs. Campbell told him.

"My mother knows you," the policeman said. "You

can go this time. But you really should come to a full stop at Harrison Street!"

* * * * *

What did Mrs. Campbell do wrong? What difference did it make that the policeman's mother knew her? Why are names important? Does the Creator of the universe know *your* name? How do you know that Jesus loves you?

My response:

Are you afraid about something? What difference does it make if Jesus knows you?

Boy or Girl

3

What God says:

There is neither Jew nor Greek, slave nor free, male nor female, for you are all one in Christ Jesus.

Galatians 3:28

I think about it:

In the early 1970's, a group of tourists in the capital were completing their tour of the Federal Bureau of Investigation (FBI).

The last item on the tour was a demonstration of accuracy on the firing range. In a darkened room, an Agent fired a round of shots at a paper target.

"Let's see how well I did," the Agent said, as the lights went back on. Naturally, he did very well indeed. The center of the target was filled with bullet holes.

The Agent looked around the group of tourists and handed the target to a boy in the front row.

Suddenly, the stillness of the moment was broken by the voice of another child. "I was just wondering, Sir," she said. "Do you ever give the target to a *girl?*"

* * * * *

Should a person have special privileges because of sex? Are boys "better" than girls? Are girls "better" than boys? Does that mean that everyone is exactly alike? What do you think the Bible means when it says that men and women are "one" in Jesus Christ?

My response:

Who chose your sex? Did God get what He wanted? Praise Him for what you are!

When You Grow Up

4

What God says:

In his heart a man plans his course, but the Lord determines his steps.

Proverbs 16:9

I think about it:

After an assembly which presented a number of career possibilities, two sixth graders were talking.

"I'd like to be a lawyer," Megan said. "I'm glad I don't have to be a nurse just because I'm a girl."

"Nurses can usually get jobs, Andrea said. "By the time we're old enough, the world might be full of lawyers!"

* * * * *

Time always brings changes. Some changes are the

result of unexpected things which happen to everybody all through life. When things change or "go wrong," some people complain or quit. But others seem to grow stronger. Who is in control of life's circumstances? Can you control how you will react to change? How can Jesus help you?

My response:

The next time your plans are changed, watch how you respond. Do you want to go through life reacting this way?

Lending to Jesus

5

What God says:

He who is kind to the poor lends to the Lord, and he will reward him for what he has done.

Proverbs 19:17

I think about it:

"Many people in Haiti have nowhere to turn," the missionary said. "Even by working long hours, they can't earn enough to send their children to school."

"But if the kids can't get an education, they'll always live in poverty! It's hopeless," Sally said.

"That's why the sponsorship program is so beautiful," the missionary explained. "The dollars you send every month provide school, a hot lunch, clothing, and Christian training. You can change the world for one child."

* * * * *

Are all poor people lazy? Does your family or your

church do anything to help people who live in poverty? What do they need besides money?

My response:

If the Lord asked to borrow money, would you lend it to Him?

Do's and Don'ts

6

What God says:

So whether you eat or drink or whatever you do, do it all for the glory of God.

1 Corinthians 10:31

I think about it:

Mrs. Blasco asked the girls in her Sunday school class to share some of their family rules.

"We have to pass food to the head of the table before we take any," said Joan.

"My mother thinks girls shouldn't call boys on the telephone," said Gail. "That's what *her* mother taught her."

"We aren't allowed to eat chicken with our fingers," said Brenda.

"My grandmother thinks it's wrong to sit on a bed," Tammy said.

"My father says boys and men are supposed to walk

15

on the sidewalk nearest the street," Kelly said.

"We aren't allowed to go to the movies," said Wendy.

"OK," Mrs. Blasco said. "I'm sure you get the idea. Are rules the same in every family?"

The girls giggled.

"Now, are all rules the same? Is sitting on a bed wrong in the same way telling a lie is wrong?" Mrs. Blasco asked.

The girls shook their heads.

"That's what you think," Tammy said. "You don't know my grandmother!"

* * * * *

Does *your* family have many rules? Why are rules different in different families? Do you have to obey another family's rules? Should you make fun of them? Do all Christians agree that we should glorify God?

My response:

Ask the Lord to teach you respect for the rules and opinions of others. How can you glorify Jesus in what you do today?

Handling Anger

7

What God says:

Do not let the sun go down while you are still angry.
Ephesians 4:26

I think about it:

"But what I told Marilyn was private!" Candy said.

"I don't think she meant any harm," said Rachael. "She just asked us to pray about it."

"She's no longer a friend of mine," Candy stated. "I can't trust Marilyn, and that's that."

Will the problem be solved if Candy just tries to forget about her feelings? Will it be solved if she talks to Jennifer or Debby or Sara or Mrs. Atkins? How about if she talks to Marilyn? Actually, she did, and this is what happened:

"I feel like I don't want you for a friend any more

because I can't trust you!"

"I'm sorry," Marilyn said. "At the time, I thought the Lord wanted me to get more prayer support. Please forgive me for hurting you!"

"I do forgive you," Candy said. She smiled. "You know, it's funny, but I feel closer to you than I ever did before."

My response:

Do you have anger or resentment inside that's keeping you away from someone? Will you talk it over before another day goes by?

Two Sides of Forgiveness

8

What God Says:

Forgive and you will be forgiven.

Luke 6:37

I think about it:

"You promised you wouldn't tell!" Susie said.

Becky looked down at the floor. "I'm sorry," she said.

"I thought you were my best friend," Susie protested.

"I am your best friend," Becky said. "And you're mine."

"Well, best friends don't tell each other's secrets."

"I know." Becky looked miserable. "I won't do it again."

"What makes you think I'll ever tell you a secret again?" Susie asked.

19

"I said I was sorry. What else can I do?" Becky said.

"I guess it's OK," Susie said. "Let's forget about it and still be friends."

"Not that way," Becky said. "It *wasn't* OK! I need to be forgiven."

"OK," Susie grinned. "I forgive you. By the way, I guess I need forgiveness myself. I called you a Big Blabber Mouth!"

* * * * *

Is telling somebody "it's OK" or "it doesn't really matter" the same thing as forgiveness? Practice saying (out loud), "Please forgive me," and "I forgive you." Which is easier for you to do? How does it feel when somebody won't forgive you? Will Jesus forgive you if you won't forgive others?

My response:

Ask Jesus to teach you more about forgiveness.

Don't Give Up

9

What God says:

Encourage one another daily, as long as it is called Today, so that none of you may be hardened by sin's deceitfulness.

Hebrews 3:13

I think about it:

Listen to the voices of some discouraged people:

"What's the use? No matter how hard I try, I just can't do it."

"I hate school. Nobody likes me."

"We used to live in such a nice house."

"I'm just waiting for the time when I can get away from here and start over."

"I thought being a Christian would make a difference."

"Sure, I could do better too, if my mom wasn't drunk half the time!"

"I'm too tired."

"I'm too old."

"I'm too young."

* * * * *

Does everybody (including Christians) need encouragement? How often? Think of people who encourage you. How do they do it? Is encouragement *personal?* Are some people better at encouraging than others? How can a person improve?

My response:

Ask the Lord to show you one person you can encourage today. Then let Him show you how to do it! How did you feel?

A Joyful Sound

10

What God says:

Sing to God, sing praise to his name, extol him who rides on the clouds—his name is the Lord—and rejoice before him.

Psalm 68:4

I think about it:

Walter hated Monday mornings. Not that he didn't like school. He just liked the weekends better.

He had just returned from the shower when he heard sounds in the kitchen. The voice was singing "All hail, King Jesus." It kept getting louder and louder. Walter smiled. As he buttoned his shirt, he started singing along.

"I love to hear you sing," Walter told his mother. "It makes me feel that this is going to be a good day after all!"

"Good," his mother said. "Maybe I'll join the choir!"

23

They both laughed. Nobody in the family sang well enough for that!

* * * * *

Did Walter's mother have a "good" voice? Did she need to have perfect pitch and be able to read music in order to praise the Lord? What did she need? Why do you think Walter felt happy?

My response:

Do you sing well enough to praise the Lord? Will you do it?

Too Young?

11

What God says:

"From the lips of children and infants you have ordained praise."

Matthew 21:16

I think about it:

Tim was the youngest in a family of six children. It seemed as if everybody in the world could do more than he could.

"When you get older," his brother would promise.

"I'm sorry, but we think you're too young," his father would say.

At the Christmas pageant, Tim had to wear a dumb angel costume. And then, when they were climbing on the stage, Sandra Philpot made a face at him, and everybody laughed.

But when the evening was over, Tim felt marvelous. Everybody said that, when it came to praising Jesus, the young angels were best of all!

* * * * *

What makes the praise of children so special? Do all infants and children praise Jesus? Do you ever get tired of being "too young?" Will you do something that Jesus says you're qualified for—praise Him?

My response:

Why not praise Him now?

When We Aren't Looking

12

What God says:

When Jacob awoke from his sleep, he thought, "Surely the Lord is in this place, and I was not aware of it."
Genesis 28:16

I think about it:

Marcy Bennett's mother was beautiful and talented. She could do everything from running an advertising agency to baking flaky pie crust. But Marcy's mother didn't believe in God, and she didn't go to church.

Last winter, when Mrs. Bennett was expecting her third child, she developed physical problems which forced her to spend almost six months in bed.

"At first I could hardly make it through an hour," she said. "I read to make the time go faster. It was the first time I ever read the New Testament. And then I met Jesus!" By the time Marcy's brother John was born, Mrs. Bennett had become a Christian.

* * * * *

Do you look for the Lord in happy times? He's in them! But He's also in the difficult ones. He teaches us many lessons—even when we don't always know He's doing it!

My response:

What is the Lord teaching you today?

Words and Deeds

13

What God says:

Faith by itself, if it is not accompanied by action, is dead.

James 2:17

I think about it:

"Tell me about your friends," Grandma Brown said.

"Having friends is very important to me," Brian told his grandmother. "Friends have fun with you. They listen when you have troubles." He smiled. "My best friend is named Keith Bradley. I hope you can meet him."

"I have four best friends," Brenda said. "We have a club that meets every Tuesday. On that day, we all wear something navy blue."

"How about you, Grandma?" Brian asked.

"My best friend's name is Violet," she said. "Violet moved into the retirement village the same week I did.

Even though she never married, we have a lot in common. Mostly, we both love to read."

*　*　*　*　*

Do you think friendship is important to Grandma Brown, Brian, and Brenda? What would you think if somebody said, "I believe in friendship, but I don't have time for friends"? Or, "I think reading is lots of fun, but I don't like books"? Or, "Loving God is Number One in my life, but I don't have time to help other people"? Or "Jesus is my Savior, but I don't particularly enjoy being with Christians"?

Does what a person really *believes* become a part of what he/she *does?*

My response:

Does your life illustrate what you believe about Jesus?

Bumper Crop

14

What God says:

Remember this: Whoever sows sparingly will also reap sparingly, and whoever sows generously will also reap generously.

2 Corinthians 9:6

I think about it:

Last year, Aunt Margaret, an unmarried woman in her eighties, moved from her much-loved home into Friendship Village, a life-care center. There she began to teach a weekly Bible study. When her health became poor, she was forced to move from her apartment into a bed in the nursing care center.

Nurses are amazed at the number of visitors Margaret has. Not only do her brothers and sisters come, but she has a constant flow of nieces and nephews. And, in between times, she is visited by other residents of Friendship Village.

Without reading more of Aunt Margaret's story, what do you know about her? Do you think she complains and feels sorry for herself? What is she reaping? Based on what you've read, what do you think she sowed? How much did she sow? Name some things a person your age can sow.

My response:

Think about what you are sowing now. Are you happy about it? Will you have a good harvest?

What Love Is Like

15

What God says:

Love is patient, love is kind. It does not envy, it does not boast, it is not proud.

> *1 Corinthians 13:4*

I think about it:

"I love Gretchen, but I wish she'd stop interrupting me," Rachael said. "She always has to be the center of attention."

"I know," said Nicole. "But at least she doesn't act like a baby—like one person I could mention!"

"Frankly, I think it's because Amy's so fat," the first girl replied. "But have you noticed how much she eats! No wonder her clothes look so bad."

"Right!" said Nicole. "And then there's Beth! Lucky

Beth! She can eat anything and still look like a model. What I wouldn't give for a figure like that!"

"You do all right," said Rachael. "Personally, I thought our outfits looked better than anybody else at our lunch table."

"You know, I really love our gang! Did you see Denise sitting all alone? I'll bet she wishes she could be cool!"

* * * * *

Do you think Rachael and Nicole really *love* their friends? Does casual conversation look "worse" when you see it written down? Do you have faults? Does Jesus love and accept you the way you are?

My response:

When you say you "love" somebody, will you try to mean it? Ask the Lord to show you someone today who needs love.

Join the Angels

16

What God says:

In the same way, I tell you, there is rejoicing in the presence of the angels of God over one sinner who repents.

Luke 15:10

I think about it:

Mark Allen was obnoxious. Although his Christian parents made him come to Sunday school every week, everybody knew he didn't really want to be there.

Like many unhappy kids, Mark Allen had no friends. He wasn't bad enough to fit in with bad kids at school. But the Christian kids couldn't stand him.

Then, one Monday, Mark Allen realized—really knew in his heart—that Jesus had died to save *him.*

* * * * *

What did the angels in Heaven do? Do you think Mark

35

Allen's behavior changed right away? Do you think he suddenly had more friends? How do you think the Christian kids responded? Did Jesus love Mark Allen all along?

My response:

Ask the Lord to give you the same love for others that Jesus has!

What's Inside?

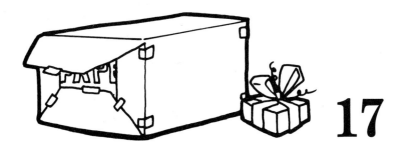

17

What God says:

The Lord does not look at the things man looks at. Man looks at the outward appearance, but the Lord looks at the heart.

1 Samuel 16:7

I think about it:

Since the department store didn't supply boxes for all of her purchases, Mrs. Benson had to use several old boxes when she wrapped the family Christmas gifts.

Because it was the correct size, an old toilet paper carton was used for Stephanie's new VCR. And, as a joke, Mrs. Benson wrapped up a can of sardines in a gold box from an expensive jewelry store.

Stephanie didn't look too thrilled when she pulled off the paper from the carton. "Well," she laughed, "I guess I'll always need it, and I'll be glad to share!" How surprised she was later!

On the other hand, she got all excited when she first saw the jewelry box. But later she said, "You can have this Dad. I don't really like sardines!"

*   *   *   *   *

Are people kind of like the Christmas gifts? Do you know somebody who looks attractive but who's ugly inside? How about someone who looks plain or unattractive but who is really warm and loving? Can you tell Christians by the way they look? Can Jesus tell?

My response:

Will you give someone the chance to be known for who he/she really is?

Always

18

What God says:

"And surely I will be with you always, to the very end of the age."

Matthew 28:20

I think about it:

"I promise to be your friend always," Ann told Beth.

"What if the kids call me names?" Beth answered.

"I'll still be your friend," Ann said.

"What if I move away?" Beth asked.

"I'll write you letters and come to visit you," answered Ann.

"What if I get sick and all my hair falls out?" Beth asked.

"I'll always be your friend," promised Ann.

"What if I'm the worst in spelling?" asked Beth.

"I'll always be your friend," Ann said.

"What if I ask Karen to my birthday party and don't

invite you?" Beth asked.

"Then you won't need me," Ann replied. You'll have Karen."

* * * * *

Has somebody promised you something and then let you down? Why is *always* a hard promise for people to keep? How are the Lord's promises different from those people make? What does Jesus promise in this verse? Can He do it? How does that make you feel?

My response:

If you're glad the Lord won't ever leave you, why not tell Him?

Instead of Fear

19

What God says:

"Don't be afraid; just believe."

Mark 5:36

I think about it:

In "Sound of Music," Julie Andrews taught the children to conquer fear by remembering their "favorite things." In other words, the children learned to substitute happy thoughts for scary ones.

Jesus tells you to conquer fear by belief in Him! Instead of thinking about whatever frightens you, you can think about Jesus who loves you and has the power to help you.

* * * * *

Are you ever afraid? What are some things that scare you? Does thinking about "favorite things" help? Have you tried trusting Jesus? He will help you overcome your fear. Just pray thanking Him for being with you and giving you courage.

My response:

Tell Jesus what you're afraid of today. How can He help? Can you picture Him taking care of it? How do you feel now?

Afraid?

20

What God says:

Do not be afraid or terrified, for the Lord your God goes with you; he will never leave you nor forsake you.

Deuteronomy 31:6

I think about it:

When Diane's father told the family that he was being transferred, at first everyone was upset.

"I like it here," Diane said. "What if I have trouble making friends?"

"I hear it's very expensive to live in that town," Diane's mother said. "What if we won't be able to get a nice house?"

"What if I can't make the team at the new school?" said Diane's brother.

"I'll be OK," said little Timmy. "You'll be there, won't you, Daddy?"

What scares you? Does Jesus know what's going to happen? Does He have power to help you? How long will He stay with you?

My response:

If you're afraid, tell Jesus about it.

A Happy Ending

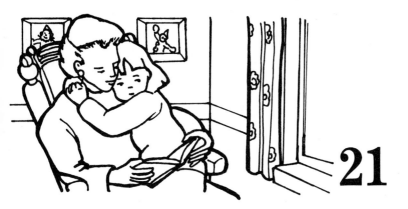

21

What God says:

Surely goodness and love will follow me all the days of my life, and I will dwell in the house of the Lord forever.
Psalm 23:6

I think about it:

Mrs. Cummings put the book down on her lap. "I hope you aren't afraid," she said. "I didn't realize this story would be so scary."

"I'm not scared," Paula replied. "It will turn out OK."

"Has someone read this book to you before?" Mrs. Cummings asked.

"No," said Paula. "But books for kids my age always have happy endings."

* * * * *

What are adventures? Think of something that happened to you that might be considered an adventure.

Are "adventures" always fun while they're happening? Do bad things sometimes happen to good people? How can you be sure your life will have a "happy ending"?

My response:

This verse is the happy ending of the Twenty Third Psalm. Do you want to memorize it?

Guardian Angels

22

What God says:

For he will command his angels concerning you to guard you in all your ways.

Psalm 91:11

I think about it:

Long ago, even before your grandparents' time, some people argued over how many angels could dance on the point of a pin! It was, of course, a puzzle with no solution.

Nobody knows for sure what angels look like! Are they invisible? Are they fat babies with wings and halos? Are they tall singers wearing white robes? Do they look like Michael Landon in TV's *Highway to Heaven?* We just don't know!

The Bible tells about many angels who seem to look

like ordinary people. It also says that angels are "good" because they are on God's side.

*   *   *   *   *

What do you think about having a guardian angel? What are some other ways the Lord guards your ways and keeps you safe? Do you need all the help you can get?

My response:

Thank the Lord for his protection.

Recognizing Jesus

23

What God says:

She turned around and saw Jesus standing there, but she did not realize that it was Jesus.

John 20:14

I think about it:

"Be careful. There's a car coming!"

"You did such a nice job!"

"Your smile lit up the stage!"

"Thank you for your kindness!"

"You should see a doctor!"

"I love you very much!"

* * * * *

When you hear loving things, encouraging things, helpful things, Jesus may be talking to you through other people. When somebody gives you something you need, Jesus may be using that person in your life. Sometimes He uses your voice or your hands too! When He does, do you want the credit?

My response:

Try to recognize Jesus in your life today.

The Best Gift

24

What God says:

For the wages of sin is death, but the gift of God is eternal life in Christ Jesus our Lord.

Romans 6:23

I think about it:

At Christmas time, one of Peter's friends came over for a cup of cocoa. Dozens of gifts were piled under the Christmas tree.

"You sure get a lot of presents," Mike said. "I didn't know you were that good!"

"Don't tell Santa Claus," Peter laughed. "Fortunately, in my family we don't always get what we deserve!"

*　*　*　*　*

Does God make a list and check it twice to find out who's naughty and nice? If eternal life were awarded to those who deserved it, who would receive the gift? Is it fair for God to give eternal life to some people and not to others? How does He decide? Why is the Gospel *Good News?*

My response:

Have you received God's gift through Jesus Christ? If not, you can! Will you talk to the Lord about it today?

Rewards and Gifts

25

What God says:

*For it is by grace you have been saved, through faith—
and this not from yourselves, it is the gift of God—not by
works, so that no one can boast.*

Ephesians 2:8, 9

I think about it:

The first year Vanessa had a garden, she planted
what she called "vegetable soup"—peas, beans, onions,
carrots, corn, and tomatoes.

"If I work hard, I may win a prize at the county fair,"
she said.

Although she didn't get a blue ribbon, Vanessa did
win second place.

"It was worth all the effort," she smiled.

"Now the real work begins," her mother said. "Next week we start canning!"

* * * * *

Did Vanessa earn the ribbon? Who provided sunshine for all the gardeners? Did they earn it? Think of some more of God's gifts. Can any of them be earned? Why do you think some people try to earn salvation? Can they do it?

My response:

Have you received salvation? Did you earn it? Thank Jesus for this precious gift!

The Only Way

26

What God says:

Jesus answered, "I am the way and the truth and the life. No one comes to the Father except through me."
John 14:6

I think about it:

"Religions are all the same," Paula said. "The important thing is to believe in God."

"That isn't what the Bible teaches," Nicole said. "Jesus isn't just one way to God. He's the *only way.*"

"That's the trouble with you," Paula said. "You think you know all the answers."

"I guess you'll have to read it for yourself," Paula said.

* * * * *

Does the Holy Bible have all the answers to everything? Does it answer important questions people have about God? What if people don't agree? How can you encourage them to love Jesus and read God's Word to learn how He wants them to live?

My response:

Can you talk people into belief? Are *you* a believer in Jesus? Thank Him for faith!

How to Be Forgiven

27

What God says:

If we confess our sins, he is faithful and just and will forgive us our sins and purify us from all unrighteousness.

1 John 1:9

I think about it:

On Tuesday, Steve saw a dollar on the table in the hall. He walked past it six times. But the seventh time, he reached out and picked it up.

That evening Steve's mother didn't say anything about the money. "You're awfully quiet. Is something wrong?" she asked.

Steve almost told her. But he didn't. He was embarrassed. He didn't want her to think he couldn't be trusted. When his mother went upstairs, he took the money out of his pocket and put it back.

* * * * *

How do you think the story ended? Was this a mistake or was it a sin? Why? Why is it hard for people to admit sins and mistakes? If sins aren't confessed and forgiven, what can happen? Is God always ready to forgive? How long does it take him to do it? What do you have to do?

My response:

Do you have something to confess? Do it now! Thank the Lord that He is fair, and faithful, and forgiving.

All Included

28

What God says:

All have sinned and fall short of the glory of God.
                                        Romans 3:23

I think about it:

A baseball record unlikely to be broken was set by
pitcher Charles "Old Hoss" Radbourne in 1884. He
pitched seventy-two games for Providence, thirty-eight
of them in a row, and won sixty of them!

Few pitchers today win more than twenty games
during a season. Does a pitcher throw all strikes? Does
any batter get a home run every time? Are even the
best players "perfect"?

* * * * *

The Bible tells us that people who aren't perfect are
called sinners. And it says that nobody's perfect. Are
some people better than others? Why is it hard for

some people to admit that they are "sinners"? Why do people who aren't perfect need Jesus?

My response:

Has Jesus taken away your sin? Thank Him! He died to save you from your sins. He loves you very much. Tell Him how much you love Him.

It's Yours! Open It!

29

What God says:

"Anyone who will not receive the kingdom of God like a little child will never enter it."

Luke 18:17

I think about it:

"I have something for you," Mr. Jennings told his small daughter. He handed Marcy a present wrapped in blue paper. She pulled off the paper and squealed with delight at the new book.

"I have something for you, too," Mr. Jennings told his wife.

She looked at the brown wrapping. "I can't eat candy," she said. "I'm on a diet."

"It isn't candy," Mr. Jennings said.

"You don't usually bring me presents. What's wrong?" she asked.

"Nothing's wrong," Mr. Jennings said.

Finally, she pulled off the rest of the paper. "Oh, dear," she said. "This must have cost a fortune. Are you sure we can afford it?"

* * * * *

How do you think Mr. Jennings felt? Would a loving father offer his family a gift of something *bad?* Does God *want* people to receive the kingdom of God? Why do some of them have a hard time accepting it?

My response:

Have you trusted Jesus enough to receive His gift of eternal life? Thank Him for it!

What Faith Is

AIRPORT GATE 3

30

What God says:

Now faith is being sure of what we hope for and certain of what we do not see.

Hebrews 11:1

I think about it:

Every summer since his father died, Andrew flew alone to visit his grandmother in Houston. It was the best adventure in the entire year.

Last year, when he was eleven, Andrew scanned the waiting room. He looked again. But no one was there to meet him.

An airline representative escorted Andrew to a special room for children flying alone.

"I'm supposed to wait for Grandma Jane," Andrew said. "Will she know where I am?"

Assured that his grandmother would be told of his whereabouts, Andrew began to enjoy the games.

Shelly, ten, from Indianapolis, was anxiously waiting for her father. "Are you sure they'll come?" she asked.

"I can count on Grandma Jane," Andrew said. "I hope she comes soon so I can see the oil rigs on my way to her house."

"Hi, Andrew!" a smiling woman said. "You won't believe the traffic jam getting into the airport! It's as bad as Christmas!"

Right behind her was a tall man. "Hi, Shelly," he said, hugging his daughter.

* * * * *

Andrew had faith in his grandmother. He was certain she'd come for him. Did he have to worry about transportation to her house? Did he have to worry about anything? What did he have to do?

When you have faith in Jesus, what do you have to do? Who is in charge? Do you have to worry about anything?

My response:

Will you have faith in Jesus today? How about next week? How about when you're an adult?

Giving Jesus Joy

31

What God says:

The Lord delights in those who fear him, who put their hope in his unfailing love.

Psalm 146:11

I think about it:

When Jamie Beaumont first got her puppy, the Beaumonts wondered if they had made a mistake. Although Mindy was cute looking, she barked all the time, jumped on people, and ran away every chance she got.

"This won't do," Mr. Beaumont said. "Mindy will have to go to obedience school."

At first it was hard. Mindy wanted her own way. But gradually the dog learned that Jamie was in charge. Jamie was to be obeyed. In time, bad habits disappeared, and Mindy even learned three tricks. Jamie was so proud of Mindy.

"Watch Mindy!" Jamie announced to the family one Sunday afternoon. "Stay, Mindy!"

While the family watched, the puppy didn't move—even when Jamie left the room.

"What a terrific dog!" Mr. Beaumont said.

"I love you, Mindy!" Jamie said, when she returned with a treat. The dog didn't say anything. But she did wag her tail!

* * * * *

Do you think Mindy was happier when she pleased the Beaumonts? In what way did the dog fear Jamie? Was there ever a time that Jamie didn't love Mindy? What is the difference between *fearing* God and *being afraid of* God? Can you see how pleased the Lord is when you trust and obey Him?

My response:

Do you want Jesus to be Master (in charge) of your life? Talk to Him about it.

A New Spirit

32

What God says:

If anyone does not have the Spirit of Christ, he does not belong to Christ.

Romans 8:9

I will give you a new heart and put a new spirit in you.

Ezekiel 36:26a

I think about it:

Which of these young people sound like true believers in Jesus?

a) "I'm going to try my hardest to be perfect in the New Year."

b) "I want to do my best in the New Year, and I'm asking Jesus to help me."

c) "I don't see anything wrong in paying him back for what he did."

d) "Sometimes I am tempted to do the wrong thing."

e) "I used to act bad most of the time! Now, I actually don't want to act that way any more!"

f) "I hate him, and I always will!"

g) "I forgive you."

* * * * *

What difference does it make when Jesus comes to live in your heart? Is He alive? How do you know? Do you feel different? What does the Bible say?

My response:

If you aren't sure you belong to Christ, talk with a Christian about it. If Jesus lives in your heart, will you "walk with Him and talk with Him" today?

Member of the Family

33

What God says:

The Lord disciplines those he loves, as a father the son he delights in.

Proverbs 3:12

I think about it:

Art and his mother were alone for two years after Art's father died. When his mother married again, he not only had a new "father" but also two "brothers." Even though he tried, Art could not seem to feel part of the new family.

"You're spoiled, that's what," Peter told him.

"Yeah," Paul said. "You're used to being the big cheese."

"I hate you both," Art said. He swung at Paul, shoved Peter aside, and went to his room.

"OK, boys," Mr. Paulson said. "This bickering has to stop! Peter and Paul, you're grounded for the weekend." Then he looked at Art. "And Art, you're grounded too! I can't have my sons fighting all the time!"

It was the first time his new father had punished him.

"That's when I knew he accepted me," Art told his mother later. "He finally treated me just like the others."

* * * * *

How does punishment show a parent's love? When and how does the Lord discipline people? Is everything bad that happens punishment from God? (See John 9:1, 2.) If God disciplines you, does He stop loving you?

My response:

Are you glad you're one of God's children? Tell Him!

What Can I Do?

34

What God says:

"I am the vine; you are the branches. If a man remains in me and I in him, he will bear much fruit; apart from me you can do nothing."

John 15:5

I think about it:

During Christmas vacation, Andy's father took him to his office so he could help with a special project. As soon as they arrived, the phone rang, and Andy was left alone. He hung up his coat and walked around to look at the computer terminals. Then he found a typewriter, inserted paper, and wrote a letter to his brother.

"Sorry, Andy," his father said, when he returned. "It was a long distance call from a customer in Chicago. Come over here and I'll show you what I want you to do."

When the next call came in, Andy was busy sorting cards into alphabetical order. "This is fun," he said later. "I couldn't do anything until you showed me what to do and how to do it."

* * * * *

What did Andy mean? Is it true that Andy could do *nothing?* Without the Lord's help and direction, can't you do *anything?* Can a branch keep growing and bearing fruit once it's cut off from its vine? What does this show you about keeping connected to Jesus?

My response:

Tell Jesus to show you what He wants you to do today. If you ask, He'll even help you do it!

Don't Forget

35

What God says:

I have hidden your word in my heart that I might not sin against you.

Psalm 119:11

I think about it:

"I'm getting more and more forgetful," said Grandma Rose. "But I can remember the three most important things."

"Please tell me the important things," Amanda said.

"Well, first, I remember the Twenty-Third Psalm," her grandmother said. "I learned it when I was a young girl."

"What are the other two things?" Amanda wondered.

"What other two things?" the old woman asked.

* * * * *

Do you know someone who forgets things? Are they

usually important things? Does it really matter? What have you memorized? Will everybody need the Twenty-Third Psalm?

My response:

Would you like to start memorizing Scripture? When will you start? Will Jesus help you?

Choices

36

What God says:

Test everything. Hold on to the good. Avoid every kind of evil.

1 Thessalonians 5:21, 22

I think about it:

Some kids were discussing their values:

"I decided not to hang around with Joel any more," Andy said. "Whenever I was with him, I always got into trouble."

* * * * *

"My family doesn't watch certain programs," Ann said. "We avoid TV that exploits sex."

* * * * *

"I do my homework and never skip class. After all, I plan to go to college!" said Ken.

"I don't talk dirty or swear, and I don't prefer to listen to it," Samantha said. "My friends feel the same way."

* * * * *

"I won't follow the crowd if I don't like where the crowd is going," Kate said.

* * * * *

Is it possible to avoid all evil? Can you avoid a lot of it? Is it too soon for you to make decisions about things like dating, sex, drinking, smoking, drugs? Why are the friends you choose important?

My response:

Are there decisions you'd like settled today? The Lord will help you.

Taking Sides

37

What God says:

If God is for us, who can be against us?

Romans 8:31

I think about it:

"In the 1940s a survey listed the top seven discipline problems in public schools: talking, chewing gum, making noise, running in the halls, getting out of turn in line, wearing improper clothes, not putting paper in the wastebaskets.

"A 1980s survey lists these top seven: drug abuse, alcohol abuse, pregnancy, suicide, rape, robbery, assault." *Newsweek,* January 5, 1987, page 64

* * * * *

Is life, even in the school world, getting to be a more dangerous place? Sometimes does it seem as if almost everybody is on the side of evil? Who is on the side of good? Does God have power to help? Can anything separate you from God? (See Romans 8:35-39.)

My response:

The Lord is on your side. Are you on His?

Helping the Homeless

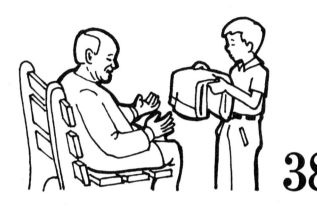

38

What God says:

He who is kind to the poor lends to the Lord, and he will reward him for what he has done.

Proverbs 19:17

I think about it:

"It was freezing cold and pouring rain. I had reached the dregs of human suffering, having lost both my wife and son. After I had long since given up, there I was, a street person. A person I had often looked upon with uncaring eyes. Suddenly, there in front of me stood a little boy with a face of spring, who gave me a respectful, "Here sir, I have a blanket for you." He had given me more than a blanket, he gave me new hope." From back cover of *Trevor's Place* by Ferrell and Waken (Harper, 1985)

The boy was Trevor Ferrell, an 11-year-old from the suburbs, who began a ministry of caring for the homeless in Philadelphia.

*   *   *   *   *

Have you seen pictures of poor people in magazines or on television? Do you think being poor is their own fault? Does Jesus blame them? Can you think of something you can do to help?

My response:

If you have a home and enough to eat, thank the Lord. Will you pray for those who don't?

Love of Money

39

What God says:

For the love of money is a root of all kinds of evil. Some people, eager for money, have wandered from the faith and pierced themselves with many griefs.

1 Timothy 6:10

I think about it:

"You've done a fine job of shoveling snow," Mr. Andrews said, as he handed each boy a $5.00 bill. "What are you fellows going to do with all your money?"

"I'm saving it," Austin replied. "I put every penny I get into my savings account at the bank."

"I'm sending some to a poor child in Haiti," Robert said. "And I want to get my mom a neat birthday present."

*　*　*　*　*

Is saving money a good goal? What's the difference

between saving and hoarding? Can a person love money too much? How can you tell if that's happening to you?

My response:

Do you love money? What is first in your life?

Giving and Receiving

40

What God says:

"It is more blessed to give than to receive."

Acts 20:35

I think about it:

The brothers were fighting over the scarce nickle in their father's change.

"I want it!" Mike said. "It's really my turn to go through the money. And don't forget, I was the one who first started collecting coins."

"But you already have one of those nickles," Andrew said.

Mike didn't say anything.

"Don't you know it's more blessed to give than to receive?" Andrew asked.

"Sure, I know it," Mike said. "That's why I want you to give it to me. I want you to be blessed!"

* * * * *

Think of a time you enjoyed *receiving* mainly because the giver wanted to please you. Now think of a time that you could hardly wait to *give* someone something. Are giving and receiving *both* pleasant? Can you have one without the other?

My response:

Ask Jesus to help you learn more about giving and receiving.

Is It Too Hard?

41

What God says:

"I am the Lord, the God of all mankind. Is anything too hard for me?

Jeremiah 32:27

I think about it:

"Dad, I need help with my math homework," Andy said.

"Sorry, Andy. I can't help you tonight."

Do you think the problems are too hard for Andy's father?

* * * * *

Richard went sledding in the new snow instead of doing his book report. That night he prayed, "Lord, please make the snow deeper so we won't have school tomorrow."

Is making more snow too hard for God? Do you think school will be cancelled?

* * * * *

"Lord, please heal my grandfather," Justin prayed.

Is healing Justin's grandfather too hard for God? Does the God who can do anything want you to ask?

My response:

Is meeting your need today too hard for God? Will you ask for His help?

A Note of Praise

42

What God says:

But let all who take refuge in you (the Lord) be glad; let them ever sing for joy.

Psalm 5:11

I think about it:

Jane Wagner, who writes the material for comedian Lily Tomlin, worked behind the scenes, without credit, for years.

When the Broadway play "In Search" opened, the audience did an unusual thing. At the conclusion of the performance, after cheering the star of the show, they began to chant, "Author, Author, Author."

Miss Wagner was pushed onto the stage to receive deafening applause.

"I don't require constant praise," Miss Wagner said. "But the recognition at that point was something I'll never forget."

God is a little like the author. Not only is He the creator of the universe, He's in charge of keeping everything going. Does He do it for praise? Do you think it pleases Him when men offer up praises to Him for who He is and what He does?

My response:

Do you want to praise Him now?

You Can Count on It!

43

What God says:

Give thanks to the Lord, for he is good. His love endures forever.

Psalm 136:1

I think about it:

"Good dog, yesterday."
"Bad dog today!"

* * * * *

"Roger was a good quarterback last year."
"Now he's bad, in fact, he's terrible!"

* * * * *

"She's a good cook most of the time."
"But when it comes to making pies, she's bad."

"Yesterday I got a good grade."
"Today I got a bad grade."

* * * * *

"God is good!" Always!

* * * * *

Most "good" changes from time to time. Also, people don't always agree on whether something is "good" or not. But have you ever heard of Jesus being called "bad"? How long will His love last?

My response:

Isn't it wonderful to know you can count on God's goodness and love? Praise Him!

Don't Worry

44

What God says:

Cast all your anxiety on him because he cares for you.
1 Peter 5:7

I think about it:

"Will you be checking all your luggage?" asked the airline representative.

"Everything except this one," Mrs. Jones said.

"Are you sure you can handle it?" Mr. Jones asked. "You have to change planes in St. Louis."

"I can handle it," Mrs. Jones said. "I can't trust it to anyone else."

The suitcase was so heavy Mrs. Jones couldn't lift it into the overhead compartment of the plane. A flight attendant had to help. When they reached St. Louis, other passengers became angry when they had to wait while Mrs. Jones struggled down the aisle.

It *was* far between gates. Mrs. Jones thought her

arm would break. Once she fell down and tore her stocking. Long before she claimed her other luggage in Colorado Springs, Mrs. Jones decided to accept help. Next time she's going to check everything.

*   *   *   *   *

Is it possible to trust the Lord for most things and still keep some problems for yourself? Is the Lord able to handle everything? Is He willing to do it? Why do you think a Christian might worry?

My response:

Will you trust everything to the Lord? Tell Him about it, and then thank Him.

Wanting More

45

What God says:

But godliness with contentment is great gain.
1 Timothy 6:6

I think about it:

On Christmas, after the other gifts had been opened, Grandpa Roy reached into his pocket and pulled out a handful of envelopes.

"Here's a check for each of you," he said. "There's always something you want."

Grandpa Roy does (and says) the same thing every year.

This year, Tim had just opened a mountain of toys— everything he asked for, and more.

Randy had just received a 10-speed bike.

Debbie had received so many clothes that she could wear a new outfit every day for a week.

Sean had received his own computer.

The parents of these children live in a big, expensive house. The father just bought the mother a new car. Once the holidays are over, the mother is treating them both to a cruise.

*　*　*　*　*

Do you think anybody had a hard time thinking of something to buy with his/her check? Is there always something *you* want? How much do you already have? When do you think you'll be satisfied? What is contentment? How does it help a person? When people say that "Jesus satisfies," what do you think they mean?

My response:

Are you thankful for what you have? Do you want to learn to be contented? Will you pray about it?

When Trouble Comes

46

What God says:

God is our refuge and strength, an ever present help in trouble.

Psalm 46:1

I think about it:

"Lord," Roger prayed, "I'm counting on You to help me!" Even as he was talking, Roger felt himself slip farther.

"Lord Jesus, I know I don't deserve to be found," he said. "What I did was wrong. When I disobeyed my father, I also sinned against You!"

Roger choked back a sob. His chest felt tight. "Please feel sorry for me, and do something to help me!"

Roger took a deep breath. His panic was lifting.

"Lord, thank You for being here with me!" he prayed.

At first he thought the sound was a bird. But birds don't call his name! "Roger! Roger! Roger, where are you?"

Later as they rode in the back of the station wagon, Roger's father put his arms around his son. "The Lord heard my prayer," he said. "Thank God, you're safe!"

* * * * *

Name two things Roger prayed for. Do you think he prayed at other times—when he wasn't in trouble? When you're in trouble, who can you always talk to? Do you think a lot of people pray when they're scared? Is that a reason *not to pray?* What if the trouble is really your own fault?

My response:

Are you in trouble? If not, will you remember to pray the next time trouble comes? Will you talk to Jesus in the meantime?

The True Test

ADAMS
APPLE ORCHARD

47

What God says:

"A new command I give you: Love one another. As I have loved you, so you must love one another. All men will know that you are my disciples if you love one another."
John 13:34-35

I think about it:

The Johnsons were driving through an orchard in Door County, Wisconsin.

"What kind of trees are they?" Ryan asked.

"I don't know," said Mr. Johnson. "Can you see the fruit?"

*   *   *   *   *

Christians are said to "bear fruit." What kind of fruit? In Galatians 5:22, God says the first "fruit of the Spirit" is love. (Others are: joy, peace, patience, kindness, goodness, faithfulness, gentleness and self-control.)

Do cherry trees have to try to bear cherries? It is in the new *nature* of a true Christian to be loving. Are Christians the only people who love others? Jesus says that He wants you to love other believers because that is part of your new nature. Somehow, He will convince others that you love Him.

My response:

A well-known chorus says, "They'll know we are Christians by our love." Do you think this describes your church?

RSVP

48

What God says:

I rejoiced with those who said to me, "Let us go to the house of the Lord."

Psalm 122:1

I think about it:

Consider the following invitations:

"Let's go to the movies."

"I have a ticket for the Redskins game. Want to go?"

"Grandma wants you to come for a week."

"Want to go to the mall?"

"Dad won a trip to Bermuda for the whole family."

"Want to ride along to the drug store?"

"Will you come with me to Sharon's party?"

"Wanta ride in our new convertible?"

"Let's go to church!"

* * * * *

If you had to rate your acceptances in order of preference, would you be embarrassed? Why do you go to church? Has Jesus invited you to "follow me"? What was your answer?

My response:

Are you happy about your attitude toward church? If not, how can you change it?

Children's Children

49

What God says:

May you live to see your children's children.

Psalm 128:6

I think about it:

"What's it like to be a grandpa?" William asked.

"It's very nice," said Grandpa Smith. "In fact, it's quite a pleasant surprise. Being a grandparent isn't exactly something you prepare for—like being a doctor."

"When you were a boy, did you ever think about it?" William wondered.

"Never," his grandfather said.

"Tell me about when you were a boy. What were you like?"

How does a person get to be a grandparent? Are you curious about what your children will be like? What kind of a parent do you think you'll be? If you have grandparents, how much time do you spend with them? Could you spend more if you wanted to? Have you asked them what your parents were like? What else could they tell you?

My response:

If you have grandparents, think about how special you must be to them! Would you like to get better acquainted? If you don't have grandparents, is there an older person you could "adopt"?

Try It

50

What God says:

*Taste and see that the Lord is good; blessed is the man
who takes refuge in him.*

Psalm 34:8

I think about it:

"Yuck!" Justin said. "I don't see how anybody can eat
that stuff!"

Nobody paid any attention to him. For one thing,
they had heard him before. And, if Justin didn't want
to eat it, that meant more for the rest of them.

Finally, one day when nobody was looking, Justin
took a small bite. "Hey, this is good! I like it!" Naturally, nobody could believe it.

* * * * *

Are there things you don't like? Have you tried them
recently? Why do supermarkets sometimes offer free

samples? Is the Lord good – whether a person knows it or not? If you start following Jesus when you're young, will He still bring you pleasure when you're old?

My response:

Do you know that the Lord is good? Praise Him! Will you give someone else a chance to "taste and see" if the Lord is good?

Follow the Leader

51

What God says:

Whether you turn to the right or to the left, your ears will hear a voice behind you, saying, "This is the way; walk in it."

Isaiah 30:21

I think about it:

The Youngs were taking two cars to a new vacation place at the beach. Mr. Young decided to drive the Ford, and Sean followed in the Honda.

Because the first part of the trip took them through an unfamiliar part of the city, both cars drove slowly. Sean didn't want to get on the wrong road.

By afternoon, Sean had relaxed. He was speeding along the turnpike toward the ocean. He could hardly wait to see the new place and try out the rented boat.

But when Mr. Young turned off at Exit 23, Sean wasn't watching. It took about half an hour before he realized that he was no longer following his father.

* * * * *

Do you think the whole vacation was spoiled? Would Mr. Young find a way to get in touch with Sean? Can you accidentally stop following Jesus? What might distract you?

My response:

Are you pretty good at hearing the Lord's voice? When He tells you which way to go, do you always follow Him? Will you follow Him today?

Is Suffering Worth It?

52

What God says:

Endure hardship with us like a good soldier of Christ Jesus.

2 Timothy 2:3

I think about it:

During the time of the Revolutionary War, armies seldom fought during the winter. They made camp and waited for spring.

Many have read about the winter of 1778, when George Washington's army lost 2,500 men at Valley Forge.

The winter before Valley Forge and the winter afterward were spent at Jockey Hollow, near Morristown, NJ. In 1777, the year before Valley Forge, soldiers endured heavy snows, shortages of food and clothing, and a smallpox epidemic.

The winter after Valley Forge was the most severe of the century. The army endured twenty-eight snowfalls, with snow up to four feet deep. It was so cold that the Hudson and Delaware rivers were frozen solid. Again there was a lack of food, clothing, and other supplies. Some called the suffering that year even worse than Valley Forge.

* * * * *

What did George Washington's soldiers endure to secure your independence? Was it worth it? What hardships do Christians endure to follow Jesus? Is it worth it?

My response:

Are you enduring hardship today? Who will help you?

Suffering Ends

53

What God says:

And the God of all grace, who called you to his eternal glory in Christ, after you have suffered a little while, will himself restore you and make you strong, firm and steadfast.

1 Peter 5:10

I think about it:

At first, when Jennifer's father lost his job, the whole family suffered. Mr. Markem felt unappreciated and afraid he wouldn't be able to find another job. His wife felt embarrassed and afraid their money would run out. The children worried about having to move to another city and leaving their friends.

Without the large salary, the Markems had to decide the most important things to spend their money on. They learned to appreciate and encourage each other. They learned to trust God for the future. And, one day, they discovered that they were stronger than they ever had been before.

* * * * *

How did the Markems suffer? How long did they suffer? Did they become strong *after* Mr. Markem found another job? What are some other ways people suffer?

My response:

Are you suffering now? Will the pain end? What does God promise?

Quick Help

54

What God says:

I know whom I have believed, and am convinced that he is able to guard what I have entrusted to him for that day.

2 Timothy 1:12

I think about it:

"That's one of my favorite hymns!" Stephen's mother said, as she listened to his memory verses.

"I can tell," he smiled. "I didn't realize that it came from the Bible."

"Lots of hymns and choruses do," she said. "That's why they're so helpful."

"I'll tell you a short-cut with this verse," Stephen said. "Sometimes I just remind myself that *I KNOW HE IS ABLE.*"

* * * * *

When you say, "I know," there is no room for doubt.

And He (Jesus) "is able" to handle anything that comes into your life! Nothing is too hard or too easy for Him. Next time you have a problem—any problem—remember these words: I KNOW HE IS ABLE.

My response:

When you KNOW HE IS ABLE, praise Jesus!

Perfect Peace

55

What God says:

You will keep in perfect peace him whose mind is stead-fast, because he trusts in you.

Isaiah 26:3

I think about it:

Mr. Sanderson was driving down a mountain when his brakes went out.

"I felt incredibly calm," he reported. "It was almost as if Jesus was driving and I was the passenger. For what seemed like a long time, I calmly steered. I never met another vehicle.

"Then the car picked up speed, and I could feel the cold sweat on my hands. Fortunately, just then I saw the rest stop! I glided in and used the emergency brake to stop.

"At first, I was so shaky I could hardly get out of the car. But when I did, I could see for miles. It was the most beautiful sight I've ever seen. I couldn't stop praising the Lord!"

A song sung at the end of a church service says, "Jesus is the only perfect resting place. He gives perfect peace." Who does He give it to? When? Why is trusting Him necessary?

My response:

Do you have perfect peace? Do you want it? Will you trust Jesus for everything?

Tempted?

56

What God says:

When tempted, no one should say, "God is tempting me."
For God cannot be tempted by evil, nor does he tempt
anyone.

James 1:13

I think about it:

What's wrong with each of the following?

"I know I promised to babysit," Sally said. "But that
turned out to be the night of the youth group party. You
want me to have Christian friends, don't you?"

"If the Lord didn't want me to go off my diet, He
shouldn't have let Katie serve hot fudge sundaes!"

"I didn't think of it as gossip," Paul said. "It was a
prayer request."

Does God tempt anyone? Does a person have to sin? When you're tempted, who helps you resist?

My response:

What tempts you? Do you want the Lord to help you not to sin?

A Most Important List

GATE K

57

What God says:

Rejoice that your names are written in heaven.
Luke 10:20

I think about it:

Bobby was so excited he could hardly keep quiet. A man who did business with his father had invited them to sit in his box at Giant stadium.

This was no ordinary game. The Giants' games were always a sell-out, but the winner of this afternoon's game would play in the Super Bowl.

"Do you have our tickets?" Bobby asked.

"They're being held at Gate K," his father explained. "Our names are on a list."

"I wish we had tickets," Jim said. "What if we get

there, and they don't have our names?"

"They will," the father said. "I know we can count on Reggie Stahr."

* * * * *

Have you ever had your name on a list? Did you have a scary feeling that it might disappear? As soon as you become a Christian, the Lord puts your name on the list of those who can enter Heaven! (If you aren't sure you have been saved, talk to somebody who understands the Bible.) From now on, do you need to worry about it?

My response:

Rejoice! You'll spend eternity in Heaven with other Christians and Jesus! Be glad!

He Arose!

58

What God says:

The angel said to the women, "Do not be afraid, for I know that you are looking for Jesus, who was crucified. He is not here; he has risen, just as he said. Come and see the place where he lay.

Matthew 28:5, 6

I think about it:

The Johnsons were having their devotional time. Because Easter was coming soon, Mr. Johnson wanted to be sure that each of his children understood the story. "Why didn't the women find Jesus in the tomb?" he asked.

"Jesus rose from the dead," said James.

"How do you know that?" asked Mr. Johnson.

"The Bible says so," Amanda replied.

"He's alive now," Benjamin said. "I talked to Him today."

"Good!" Mr. Johnson smiled. "Now let's sing an Easter song."

Everyone joined in, even little Amy:

Low in the grave He lay—
Jesus, my savior.
Waiting the coming day—
Jesus, my Lord.

On the chorus, everyone sang loud:

Up from the grave He arose!
(Hymn written by Robert Lowry)

Afterwards, Mr. Johnson asked if they had any questions.

Amy did. "Explain it again," she said. "Just what was He doing in the gravy?"

* * * * *

Does the real Easter story have anything to do with colored eggs or rabbits? Were people surprised that Jesus was alive again? Why is Easter a happy time?

My response:

Do you know any other Easter songs? Are you glad Jesus rose from the dead? Why don't you tell Him about it?

He's Coming Back

59

What God says:

And if I go and prepare a place for you, I will come back and take you to be with me that you also may be where I am.

John 14:3

I think about it:

When Mr. Shafer took a new job in Boston, he left his family in Philadelphia. One weekend, he was joined by Mrs. Shafer, and they hunted for a home in the new location.

"We'll have a beautiful house," they told the children. "We decided to have this house built." He showed them a picture.

For months, the Shafers waited in Philadelphia.

They missed Mr. Shafer. Although he came to visit every other weekend, he spent most of his time working in Boston.

At last Mr. Shafer came to move his family to their new location. They all loved their two-story colonial home. But mostly they loved being together again!

* * * * *

Why did the family have to wait? Do you think Mr. Shafer considered not going back to get them? Why did he want his family with him? Why can't we be with Jesus right away? Will He come back for us?

My response:

Are you looking forward to the Lord's return? Praise Him for His faithfulness.

What Heaven Is Like

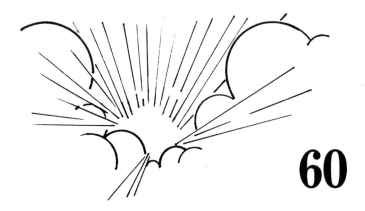

60

What God says:

He will wipe every tear from their eyes. There will be no more death or mourning or crying or pain, for the old order of things has passed away.

Revelation 21:4

I Think about it:

"Do you think Heaven will really have streets of gold and pearly gates?" Bill asked.

"I can't quite picture myself with wings and a harp and a halo," Zack laughed.

"I guess we'll have to wait and see," Dr. Forrester said. "But we do know that no one will die or get hurt or feel unhappy! It sounds pretty good to me!"

* * * * *

Have you ever wondered why life seems so hard for some people? Do you wish you could take away the pain from the family of a wonderful man who was killed in an automobile crash? How about victims of terrible diseases? God says He has planned a wonderful eternity for those who believe in Jesus!

My response:

Thank the Lord for a promised end to suffering.

My Own Devotion

What God says:

I think about it:

My response:

My Prayer List